# SNOW LEOPARDS
### AND THEIR BABIES

MARIANNE JOHNSTON

A ZOO
Life
Book

The Rosen Publishing Group's
**PowerKids Press**™
New York

*Special thanks to Diane Shapiro of the Bronx Zoo for making this project possible.*

Published in 1999 by The Rosen Publishing Group, Inc.
29 East 21st Street, New York, NY 10010

First Edition

Book Design: Resa Listort

Photo Credits: All photos © Wildlife Conservation Society.

Johnston, Marianne.
   Mother snow leopards and their babies / by Marianne Johnston.
         p.    cm.
   Includes index.
   Summary: Describes the characteristics of snow leopards and how mother snow leopards living in zoos are taught to care for their babies.
   ISBN 0-8239-5317-3
   1. Snow leopard—Juvenile literature. 2. Snow leopard—Infancy—Juvenile literature. 3. Zoo animals—Juvenile literature. [1. Snow leopard. 2. Leopard. 3. Animals—Infancy. 4. Zoo animals.] I. Title. II. Series: Johnston, Marianne. Zoo life book.
   QL737.C23C689   1998
   599.75'55—dc21
                                              98-23987
                                                CIP
                                                      AC

Manufactured in the United States of America

# CONTENTS

# THE SNOW LEOPARD

Cold mountain areas in Central Asia are the **habitat** (HA-bih-tat) of snow leopards. Countries such as Afghanistan, China, India, and Mongolia are just some of the places these beautiful cats make their homes. There are even snow leopards on Mount Everest in Nepal. Mount Everest is the tallest mountain in the world.

There is only one **species** (SPEE-sheez) of snow leopard. And, sadly, snow leopards are **endangered** (en-DAYN-jerd). Zoos all over the world are trying to save the snow leopard from becoming **extinct** (ek-STINKT).

ORDER:
CARNIVORA
FAMILY:
FELIDAE
GENUS & SPECIES:
PANTHERA UNCIA

Only about 5,000 snow leopards remain in the wild today.

# WHAT ARE SNOW LEOPARDS LIKE?

Snow leopards have warm, thick coats of fluffy gray hair. Spots of dark gray with black rings around them dot their coats. The light colors on their coats allow snow leopards to **camouflage** (KA-muh-flaj) themselves as they wander around their snowy habitat.

Snow leopards grow to be about the size of a large dog. They weigh from 60 to 100 pounds. Snow leopards have furry tails that are almost as long as their bodies. They use these long tails to balance themselves as they leap from rock to rock.

Snow leopards eat wild deer, wild sheep, goats, and sometimes birds and rabbits.

Snow leopards are very strong. They are able to jump ▶ 50 feet up to rocks so that they can look for food.

# MOMS AND BABIES IN THE WILD

Snow leopard babies are called **cubs** (KUBS). Cubs are usually born at the beginning of summer. This allows cubs enough time to grow strong before the cold winter comes. A week before a mother snow leopard gives birth, she finds a den or a cave. This is where her cubs will be born. The cubs will spend the first two or three months of their lives in the safety of the den.

Snow leopards usually have two to four cubs at a time. Cubs stay with their mother for about a year and a half. During this time, a mother snow leopard teaches her cubs to hunt. She also protects them from **predators** (PREH-duh-terz).

Snow leopard cubs are blind for the first week of life and need their moms' protection.

# SNOW LEOPARDS AT THE ZOO

About 600 snow leopards live in zoos around the world. Zookeepers and scientists make sure the snow leopard **exhibits** (eg-ZIH-bits) are a lot like the snow leopard's natural habitat.

Snow leopards are used to very cold **climates** (KLY-mits). Some zoos have big fans that help snow leopards stay cool during the summer. One zoo even has a big air conditioner for its snow leopard! Snow leopards also like trees that provide lots of shade. So most zoos make sure that their snow leopard exhibits have shady areas.

Snow leopards like steep, rocky habitats. ▶

# GIVING BIRTH AT THE ZOO

In most zoos, snow leopards have at least two places to live. During the day, when there are visitors at the zoo, snow leopards are in their exhibit areas. At night, the leopards are moved to an indoor shelter. If a snow leopard is **pregnant** (PREG-nunt), this is where she will have her cubs.

In the wild, snow leopards are alone when they give birth. Zookeepers want to make sure a mother snow leopard has the same privacy in a zoo that she would have in the wild. This means that visitors to a zoo aren't able to see a snow leopard give birth.

◀ Snow leopards in zoos might live as long as nineteen years.

# NEWBORN CUBS

When snow leopard cubs are born, they mostly sleep and **nurse** (NERS), or drink milk from their mother's body. The helpless newborns have a full coat, and they are so small that they can fit in a grown-up's hand. Sometimes zookeepers set up small cameras in the snow leopards' den. This allows zookeepers to see what is going on in the den. They can watch the cubs and their mother without disturbing them. For the first few weeks after cubs are born, the only thing zookeepers do is make sure the mother has enough food and water. This lets the mother snow leopard **bond** (BOND) with her cubs.

Zoos are breeding snow leopards because they are an endangered species. ▶

# GETTING USED TO THE ZOO

People visiting the zoo would scare snow leopard cubs. So the cubs are not brought out to the exhibit area right away. But visitors often want to see these beautiful cubs. So some zoos have televisions that are connected to cameras inside the snow leopards' den. Visitors to the zoo can watch the cubs nursing, growing, and playing without scaring them. By the time they are three months old, the cubs have been **weaned** (WEEND). This means they no longer need their mother's milk and can eat solid food.

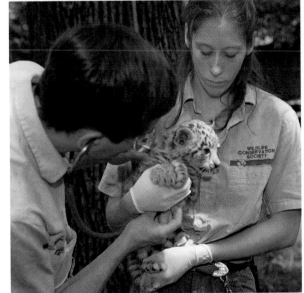

Snow leopard cubs are easily frightened by visitors.

# PROTECTING
# HER CUBS

Once snow leopard cubs are a few months old, their mother leads them out to the exhibit area. She stays very close to the cubs to protect them.

In the wild, a mother snow leopard, like many animal mothers, must protect her young from dangerous predators. A young cub could be an easy meal for a big animal.

There are no predators in a zoo for a mother snow leopard to worry about. But her **instincts** (IN-stinkts) tell her to watch her cubs very closely.

Mother snow leopards carefully protect their young cubs both in the wild and in zoos. ▶

# GROWING UP IN THE ZOO

Snow leopard cubs like to play and wrestle, just like kittens and puppies do. They stay close to their mothers. Snow leopard cubs play with her too. The cubs might even nip at their mother's tail! But the mother doesn't mind. A mother snow leopard is very **patient** (PAY-shint) and gentle with her new cubs.

By the time snow leopard cubs are two years old, they are fully grown. At this time, most zoos move the new adult snow leopards away from their mothers. Some start their own families. In the wild, it is natural for cubs to leave their mothers by this time. Adult snow leopards like to live alone.

◀ Curious snow leopard cubs like to play and explore.

# ZOOS HELPING SNOW LEOPARDS

Zoos are wonderful places to visit. It's a lot easier to go to the zoo than it is to try to see a snow leopard in the cold mountains of Central Asia. But zoos do a lot more than just let people see animals up close. Zoos are helping save animals too.

In their homeland, snow leopards are in great danger. **Poachers** (POH-cherz) kill them for their beautiful fur. Zoos provide safety for these beautiful cats. Also, snow leopards are able to raise babies safely at a zoo. By visiting zoos, you are helping to prevent snow leopards and other endangered animals from becoming extinct.

## WEB SITE

You can learn more about snow leopards at this Web site: www.mgzoo.com/snowleor.htm

# GLOSSARY

**bond** (BOND)  When a mother and her baby or babies form a close attachment to one another.

**camouflage** (KA-muh-flaj)  The color or pattern of an animal's skin or coat that helps it blend into its surroundings.

**climate** (KLY-mit)  The kind of weather a certain area has.

**cub** (KUB)  A baby snow leopard.

**endangered** (en-DAYN-jerd)  When something is in danger of no longer existing.

**exhibit** (eg-ZIH-bit)  An area of a zoo where a certain animal can be seen by visitors.

**extinct** (ek-STINKT)  When a certain kind of animal no longer exists.

**habitat** (HA-bih-tat)  The surroundings where an animal lives.

**instinct** (IN-stinkt)  Something animals are born with that guides their behavior.

**nurse** (NERS)  When a baby drinks milk from its mother's body.

**poacher** (POH-cher)  A person who illegally kills animals that are protected by the law.

**patient** (PAY-shint)  Being willing to wait for something.

**predator** (PREH-duh-ter)  An animal that kills other animals for food.

**pregnant** (PREG-nunt)  When a female has a baby or babies growing inside her.

**species** (SPEE-sheez)  A group of animals that are very much alike.

**weaned** (WEEND)  When a baby animal no longer needs to drink its mother's milk.

# INDEX